Europe

Level 9 – Gold

Helpful Hints for Reading at Home

The graphemes (written letters) and phonemes (units of sound) used throughout this series are aligned with Letters and Sounds. This offers a consistent approach to learning whether reading at home or in the classroom.

HERE ARE SOME COMMON WORDS THAT YOUR CHILD MIGHT FIND TRICKY:

water	where	would	know	thought	through	couldn't
laughed	eyes	once	we're	school	can't	our

TOP TIPS FOR HELPING YOUR CHILD TO READ:

- Encourage your child to read aloud as well as silently to themselves.
- Allow your child time to absorb the text and make comments.
- Ask simple questions about the text to assess understanding.
- Encourage your child to clarify the meaning of new vocabulary.

This book focuses on developing independence, fluency and comprehension. It is a Gold level 9 book band.

©2023 **BookLife Publishing Ltd.**
King's Lynn, Norfolk PE30 4LS, UK

ISBN 978-1-80505-058-2

All rights reserved. Printed in China.
A catalogue record for this book is available from the British Library.

Europe
Written by Shalini Vallepur
Adapted by Rebecca Phillips-Bartlett
Designed by Isabella Croker

MIX
Paper from responsible sources
FSC® C113515

Image Credits Images are courtesy of Shutterstock.com. With thanks to Getty Images, Thinkstock Photo and iStockphoto. Cover – Markus Pfaff, GoodStudio, NaMong Productions. p4–5 – Pyty, ixpert. p6–7 – Pyty, xbrchx. p8–9 – Sergey Novikov, BearFotos. p10–11 – Creative Travel Projects, ixpert, thegrimfandango. p12–13 – Pav-Pro Photography Ltd, Albert Beukhof. p14–15 – Serg64, svetkor, Olena Znak. p16–17 – Joerg Beuge, Yury Dmitrienko, Alexander Raths. p18–19 – Stuart Monk, Anna Moskvina, Daniel_Kay. p20–21 – Kite_rin, jocic.

Contents

Page 4   What Is a Continent?

Page 6   Europe

Page 8   Languages

Page 10   Weather

Page 12   Animals

Page 14   Plants and Trees

Page 16   Food

Page 18   United Kingdom

Page 20   Greece

Page 22   Index

Page 23   Questions

What Is a Continent?

A continent is a very large area of land. Our planet is split into seven different continents. Most of these continents have many countries within them.

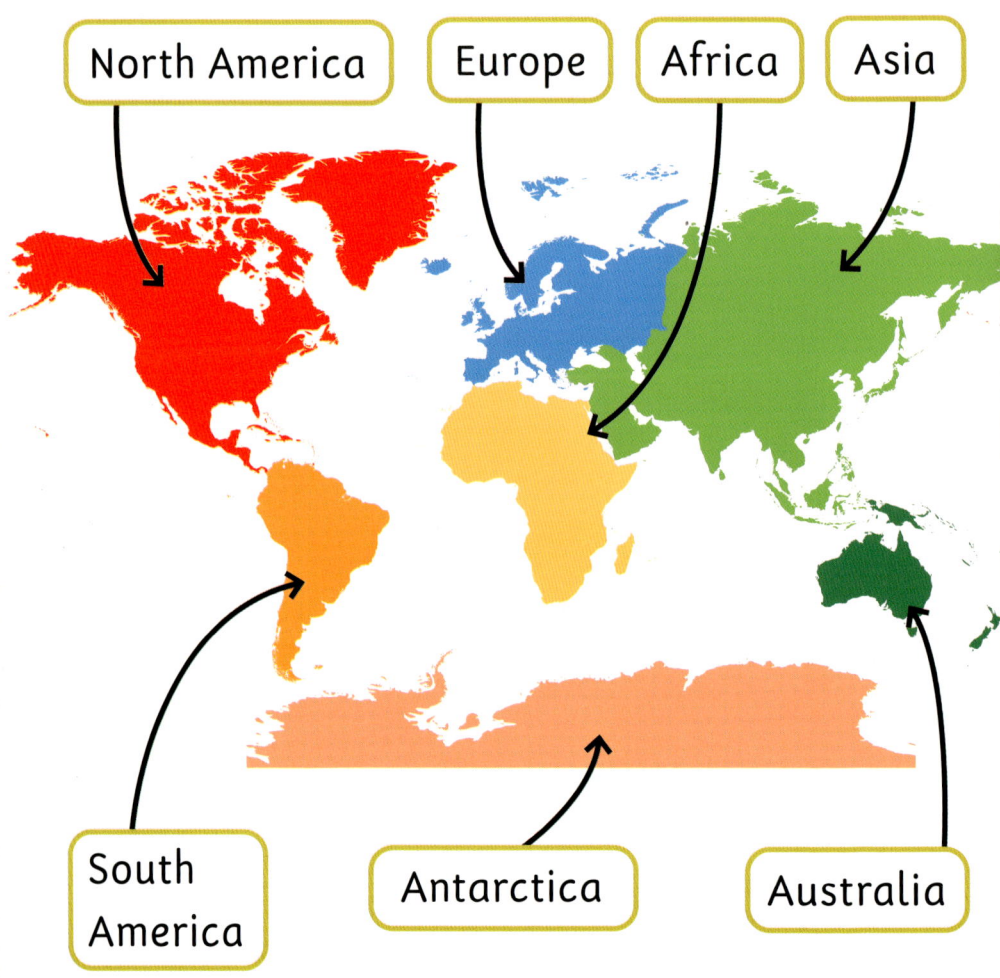

Everyone who lives on Earth lives on one of the seven continents. Each continent is very different to the others. They each have different weather and landscape and the people who live there live differently to one another.

Europe

Europe is one the seven continents. Europe is north of Africa and west of Asia. Europe is the second smallest continent, yet there are 50 countries in Europe, including France, Romania and Russia.

Europe might be small, but more than 700 million people live there! From busy cities and sunny beaches to snowy mountains, Europe has lots of different climates and landscapes. Europe is also full of amazing buildings and history.

Languages

Around 150 different languages are spoken in Europe. Some of these languages, such as English, are spoken by many people across the continent. Other languages, such as Flemish, are only spoken by people in a small part of one country.

People who live in Europe are known as Europeans. Many Europeans are bilingual. This means that they can speak and understand two languages. Many countries have an official language which is the language that most people speak.

Weather

The Equator is an invisible line that runs through the middle of the Earth. Places that are closer to the Equator are warmer than places that are farther away. Europe is north of the Equator.

Europe

The Equator

Europe has different types of weather. Europe has four seasons called winter, spring, summer and autumn. It gets colder in winter and warmer in summer. Countries in northern Europe tend to be colder than southern countries.

Snowy Finland

Sunny Italy

Animals

Many different species of animal live in Europe. Many of them have adapted to live there. Reindeer are found in the cold northern countries of Norway, Sweden, Finland, Greenland and Russia. Their thick fur coats keep them warm.

Reindeer

Many animals have clever ways of coping with the changing seasons. During winter it can be much harder for animals to find food. Animals such as mice, squirrels and hedgehogs hibernate during these months to save energy.

Squirrel

Plants and Trees

Just like animals, many plants can only live in certain areas. Pine trees have adapted to grow in cold parts of Europe. Their trunks are covered in thick bark which protects them from the harsh weather.

Pine trees

Many flowers bloom in spring and summer when it is warmer. During spring, tulips bloom in the Netherlands. In France, lavenders and sunflowers bloom during summer. As well as looking pretty, these flowers can also be used in cooking.

Food

There are millions of people in Europe, and everyone has to eat! Lots of European countries are famous for different types of food. Let's look at some tasty food from Europe! Bratwurst is a type of sausage from Germany.

Belgium is known for waffles. Belgian waffles are often served with fruit and chocolate. Bukta is a sweet bread filled with jam that comes from Hungary. For many countries, food is an important part of their culture.

Belgian waffles

Bukta

United Kingdom

The United Kingdom is made up of four countries. England, Scotland and Wales are on one island, and Northern Ireland is on another. The biggest city in the UK is London. London is also England's capital city.

London

There are lots of different landscapes in the UK. Because it is an island, the UK has lots of beaches and mountains around the coast. It also has mountains and forests that are full of wildlife.

Greece

Greece is in southeast Europe. Greece is one of the closest European countries to the Equator, so summers in Greece are very hot. Lots of people visit Greece to enjoy the hot weather.

Many people in Greece live in cities. Some people also live in villages and towns in the countryside. The tallest mountain in Greece is called Mount Olympus. This mountain is very important in Greek mythology.

Mount Olympus

Index

Equator 10, 20
Norway 12
squirrels 13
waffles 17
winter 11, 13

How to Use an Index

An index helps us to find information in a book. Each word has a set of page numbers. These page numbers are where you can find information about that word.

Page numbers

Example: balloons 5, 8–10, 19

Important word

This means page 8, page 10, and all the pages in between. Here, it means pages 8, 9 and 10.

Questions

1. How many continents are there on Earth?

2. Why do squirrels hibernate in winter?

3. What is the name of the tallest mountain in Greece?

4. Use the contents page to find out about European food.

5. Use the index page to find out what the Equator is.